Moods of
PEMBROKESHIRE
AND ITS COAST

JOHN CLEARE

HALSGROVE

First published in Great Britain in 2004

Copyright © words and pictures John Cleare 2004

Photograph opposite: At work on Mynydd Dinas (shadow self-portrait).

British Library Cataloguing-in-Publication Data
A CIP record for this title is available from the British Library

ISBN 1 84114 373 1

HALSGROVE
Halsgrove House
Lower Moor Way
Tiverton, Devon EX16 6SS
Tel: 01884 243242
Fax: 01884 243325
email: sales@halsgrove.com
website: www.halsgrove.com

Printed and bound by D'Auria Industrie Grafiche Spa, Italy

CONTENTS

DEDICATION

For Jos, my daughter, a fellow pilgrim to St David's

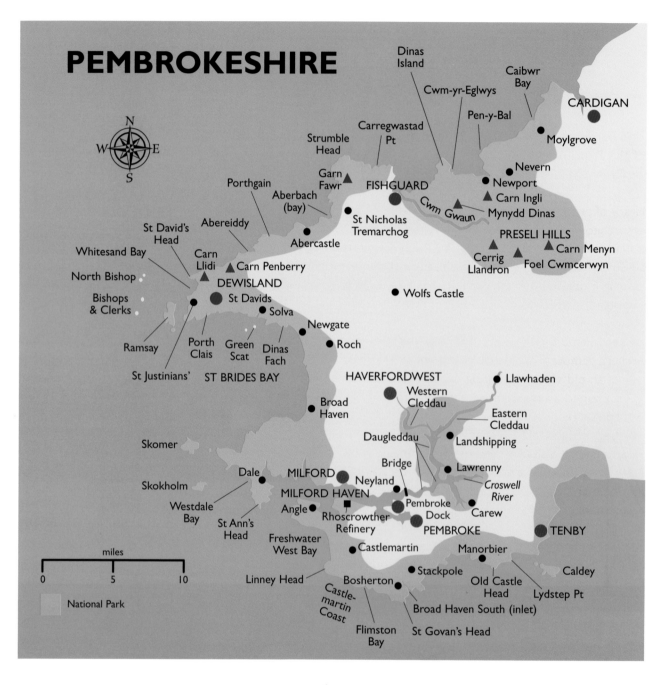

PEMBROKESHIRE

Dinas Island
Caibwr Bay
Cwm-yr-Eglwys
CARDIGAN
Pen-y-Bal
Carregwastad Pt
Moylgrove
Strumble Head
Nevern
Garn Fawr
FISHGUARD
Newport
Porthgain
Cwm Gwaun
Carn Ingli
Aberbach (bay)
St Nicholas Tremarchog
Mynydd Dinas
Abereiddy
PRESELI HILLS
St David's Head
Abercastle
Carn Menyn
Carn Llidi
Whitesand Bay
Carn Penberry
Cerrig Llandron
Foel Cwmcerwyn
North Bishop
DEWISLAND
Bishops & Clerks
St Davids
Wolfs Castle
Solva
Ramsay
Newgate
Porth Clais
Green Scat
Dinas Fach
Roch
St Justinians'
ST BRIDES BAY
HAVERFORDWEST
Llawhaden
Western Cleddau
Broad Haven
Eastern Cleddau
Skomer
Daugleddau
Landshipping
Bridge
Lawrenny
Skokholm
Dale
MILFORD
Neyland
Croswell River
MILFORD HAVEN
Westdale Bay
Angle
Pembroke Dock
Carew
St Ann's Head
Rhoscrowther Refinery
PEMBROKE
TENBY
Freshwater West Bay
Castlemartin
Manorbier
Linney Head
Stackpole
Old Castle Head
Caldey
Castle-martin Coast
Bosherton
Lydstep Pt
Broad Haven South (inlet)
Flimston Bay
St Govan's Head

miles
0   5   10

National Park

4

INTRODUCTION

*A*nglia Transwalliana they called it in medieval times – Little England beyond Wales – the far southwestern extremity of the Principality. Indeed, with the ocean on three sides and easily accessible from Ireland, Pembrokeshire has historically been the meeting place of cultures.

The legacy of prehistoric and Celt, Irish and Viking, Norman, English and Fleming flavours the landscape, the language and the very economy of this remote tip of modern Wales. Designated a National Park in 1952, its title of the Pembrokeshire Coast National Park is misleading, for although the protected area includes virtually the entire coast as a comparatively narrow strip, it also includes the Preseli Hills and the secret, drowned estuaries of the Daugleddau inland. This scenario of brooding moorland hills overlooking a mosaic of little green fields to proud cliffs, secret coves, wide beaches and a restless, island-scattered sea, make Pembrokeshire unique.

I first visited Pembrokeshire over forty years ago when with the roads being as they then were, it was *Terra Incognita*, rather more remote from London than either Holyhead or Land's End. It was winter and we drove to Tenby for the wedding of an old school chum, pushing on next day to reconnoitre the sea-cliffs near legendary St David's. As a rock-climber it seemed an opportunity too good to miss and I discovered, years later, that we had made the first modern climbing routes recorded in the county.

Several subsequent visits followed. We studied the geological map, discovered where the igneous rock met the sea and explored; limestone was then considered to be steep, loose and dangerous. It was not until my late in-laws bought a holiday home in Broadhaven that we really explored the miles of vertical limestone on the southern coast, and realised the huge potential of what is now one of the most popular sea-cliff climbing venues in Britain.

Consequently, I had ignored inland Pembrokeshire, until a photographic assignment found me in the Preseli. By a happy chance I fell in with the chief ranger of the National Park who happened to know my name. He was showing around an official American visitor and invited me to tag along. We hiked the hills, marvelled at Pentre Ifan and descended into secluded Cwm Gwaun for welcome home-brewed refreshment. I was captivated by the mood, the unspoiled ancient-ness, the sudden spikiness of these small-scale hills, so very Welsh yet unlike anything I knew elsewhere in Wales. Only later on other assignments did I discover the medieval pilgrim route from the Afon Taf to the shrine of St David, walk the picturesque Georgian streets of Tenby and admire the awesome Norman castles. I was astonished to discover the all-but-secret waterways of the Daugleddau and excited to voyage to isolated Skomer.

It is impossible to travel in Pembrokeshire without being aware of its past. To fully appreciate the county, to understand why it is what it is today, one should have an idea of its history. Some 5000 years ago Neolithic settlers scattered the area with their burial chambers. The earthen mounds which covered them have long since disappeared leaving these stark, evocative cromlech stones such as Pentre Ifan, standing typically on commanding sites, to anchor the landscape firmly in a distant and mysterious past. It was at this time that the enigmatic Stonehenge bluestones were quarried in the Preseli and transported somehow to Wiltshire. Each weighs some four tons. What long-lost skills did our remote ancestors possess?

Bronze Age folk continued to clear the forest and left their own burials mounds. The remains of settlements, field walls and forts such as that on Carn Ingli are the legacy of their druidical Celtic, Iron Age successors. Roman rule elsewhere in Britain seems to have had little impact on this remote corner of wild Wales, indeed sea-borne raids led to brief rule by Irish chieftains.

Then came Christianity, initially spread by Celtic monks also from Ireland. The fifth and sixth centuries AD are known as the 'Age of the Saints', chief among whom was St David, who died in 588 having established the church that eventually became the eponymous cathedral. There are few material remains from this period for much was destroyed by Viking marauders, but several tiny churches and inscribed stones survive together with hundred of placenames and a myriad legends.

The Vikings sacked St David's Cathedral several times, murdered its bishop in 999, frequented the magnificent anchorage of Milford Haven and settled Fishguard, Tenby and several other places. All the islands bear Norse names.

The Norman Conquest was to have a profound effect on this remote corner of Britain. When fifteen years after Hastings, William himself made a pilgrimage to St David's and accepted the local Welsh prince as a feudal vassal, it was the thin end of the wedge. By 1100 the Normans had occupied south Pembrokeshire, so easily accessible by sea, and started building castles to tighten their grip on the land, although the massive stone fortresses we admire today came a century or so later. They installed a Norman bishop to finally expunge the Celtic church and imported English – Anglo-Saxon – settlers and in due course a sizable colony of Flemings. Commerce, agriculture and especially the woollen industry flourished and not surprisingly the native Welsh tended to move out to the poorer land in the north of the country.

Thus it came to pass that even today Welsh culture, language, architecture and place names have become the norm in more rugged north Pembrokeshire while the English language, customs and architecture have predominated in the gentler south. A distinct geographical line, actually following the little Brandy Brook into the sea at Newgale Sands and known as the Landsker – a Norse word meaning 'frontier' – divided north from south. Though much blurred, this dichotomy explains much and is still very evident today.

Later history is less singular. Medieval wars and rebellions came and went. Henry Tudor – Henry VII – was born in Pembroke Castle and Henry VIII fortified Milford Haven, by then an important port for Bristol Channel, Irish and continental trade. However life for most people revolved, as it always had, around farming and the sea. In Fishguard much is still made of the 1797 French Invasion when a landing by French troops at nearby Carregwastad was defeated, so they say, by local ladies wearing their traditional red cloaks and tall black hats.

Certainly Nelson berthed his 'Wooden Walls' in Milford Haven, which he described as among the finest harbours in the world and for over century a Royal dockyard operated at Pembroke Dock: today it is a convenient terminus for car ferries to Ireland. Although transatlantic liners called only briefly at Neyland, although the RAF flying boat base has gone and Milford's once-important fishing fleet is no more, it is no surprise that the Haven is still the commercial heart of Pembrokshire. Giant supertankers have replaced the trawlers and huge oil refineries and a massive power station have sprung from its shores.

Personally I don't find these symbols of late twentieth and twenty-first century mammon particularly unsightly. The sheer scale of Milford Haven seems to swallow them up. While I object to careless oil spills – that of 1966 caused major marine pollution, albeit apparently temporary – they are a regretable fact of oil transportation. And I wish the military would move their tank ranges to a less special location and evacuate the beautiful western end of the Castlemartin Peninsula, although access is now possible in certain circumstances.

Nevertheless Pembrokeshire seems less spoilt by the malignant effects of so-called progress than most counties, than most National Parks even. Its welcoming Welshness sets it apart. The *Mabinogion*, that ancient collection of Welsh legend and folk tales, describes this far corner of the Principality as *Gwlad hud a lledrith* – the Land of Mystery and Magic. Surely anyone who loves landscape, who feels its history and has a penchant for those places where the land meets the sea will find, like me, that Pembrokeshire casts a powerful spell.

John Cleare
Fonthill, Wiltshire
March 2004

The Preseli as seen from near Haverfordwest. Foel Cwmcerwyn, the highest point at 1760 feet (536m), stands right of centre.

THE PRESELI

A feeling of times-long-past, of mystery almost, seems to shroud this roof of Pembrokeshire. Several of King Arthur's knights still remain, petrified as rocky outcrops, slain high on these strange hills by a gigantic boar. When the mists roll back, the ocean is always there along the western horizon. Indeed, the outlying craggy-crowned heights of Mynydd Dinas and Carn Ingli rise almost straight from the sea, the latter supposedly peopled by angels, encountered only by those who dare to sleep on its summit. Below in Cwm Gwaun, that long, narrow valley hidden in the folded hills, the Julian calendar is still observed, and the New Year still celebrated on January 13.

View westwards from Mynydd Dinas, a Preseli outlier, towards Fishguard harbour and town with the rocky hillocks of Garn Fawr and its satellites beyond.

The view southwards from Mynydd Dinas extends to Carn Llidi (594 ft / 181m) and the other distinctive hills around St David's.

On the Preseli crest – the view westwards along the ancient Fleming's Way towards Carn Menyn.

Autumn dawn on Cerrig Lladron and Bwlch Gwynt.

Dawn on Cerrig Lladron – view eastwards over Bwlch Gwynt towards Foel Cwmcerwyn.

Rocky Carn Breseb (c. 1060 ft / 325m) on the northern flank of the Preseli contrasts with the chequerboard farmland beyond.

Mynydd Dinas (1007 ft / 307m) looks down on the strange headland of so-called Dinas Island.

Jagged outcrops of spotted dolerite crown mysterious Carn Menyn (1198 ft / 365m), the apparent source of the Stonehenge bluestones.

Bluestones on Carn Goedog on the northern flank of the Preseli crest; Carn Ingli and Newport Bay in the distance.

This page and opposite: The cromlech at Pentre Ifan near Brynberian above Cwn Gwaun is the remains of a Neolithic burial chamber. On a balmy summer's day the great stones are imposing enough, but in inclement weather they appear brooding and mysterious.

Were these tumbled bluestones on Rhos Fach Common destined for Stonehenge? Carn Menyn stands in the distance.

An enigmatic standing stone at Tafarn-y-bwlch on the northern slopes of the Preseli.

Mountain ponies on the southern slopes of Mynydd Dinas above Cwm Gwaun.

Spring woods in Cwm Gwaun: Coed Pen-yr-allt-ddu near Pontfaen.

Beside the river in Clyn Wood, Cwm Gwaun, in early May

Sheep scamper over Rhos Fach Common below Carn Menyn.

The imposing chapel at Pontfaen in Cwm Gwaun.

Little remains of the Iron-Age hill fort on the rocky summit of Carn Ingli (1132 ft / 345m) overlooking Newport Bay.

Travellers on the road in upper Cwm Gwaun near Llanerch.

The tiny, almost-secret church of St Brynoch at Pontfaen in Cwm Gwaun is noted for its beautiful medieval wall paintings (left).

Autumn in Cwm Gwaun: Coed Sychpant on the flank of Mynydd Caregog.

Winter skyline above upper Cwm Gwaun.

Mountain stream at Pont Gelli-Fawr on the slopes of Cerrig Lladron above Cwm Gwaun.

Morning light strikes Garn Fawr crag near the summit of Mynydd Dinas.

Preseli horizons – view southeastwards from Mynydd Dinas.

Foel Cwmcerwyn, at 1760 feet (536m) is the highest point in the Preseli. View from the east over Cwm Cerwyn.

The broadest part of Cwm Gwaun lies just below Llanerch.

Gathering sheep at Tafarn-y-bwlch on the northern slopes of the Preseli above Cwm Gwaun.

The tiny church of St Gwyndaf close to the sea at Llanwnda holds relics of the French Invasion at nearby Carregwastad Point.

THE LAND

A patchwork of fields and woods and villages, the swelling landscape below the hills and behind the coast, forms the working heart of Pembrokeshire. Today it is essentially a tranquil scene though studded with frowning castles which suggest a more turbulent past. The gaunt cromlechs and standing stones scattered across the land are tokens of an earlier and more enigmatic history while the lovely cathedral rising in Dewisland – the St David's peninsula – bridges the centuries since Christianity first came to this remote corner of Wales.

The tower of St David's Cathedral rises from the little green valley of the Afon Alun.

The craggy outcrops of Carnedd lleithr, Carn Perfedd (466ft / 142m) and Carn Penberry (right – 574ft / 175m) rise over the Dewisland peninsula. They are seen here from Dowrog Common.

Carn Llidi (594ft / 181m) is the miniature mountain that rises behind St.David's Head. The lonely cottage – Llaethdy – is now a youth hostel.

Maiden Castle is one of several weird rock pinnacles on moorland above the Treffgarne Gorge at Wolfscastle.

Carew Castle stands beside the tidal creek at the head of the Carew River. It changed hands three times during the Civil War.

Manorbier Castle, high on its crag overlooking the sea, was the birthplace of Giraldus Cambrensis in 1146 and is now a private residence.

Llawhaden Castle once marked the Landsker line high up on the Eastern Cleddau.

Pembroke Castle, one of the largest in Britain, replaced an earlier fortress in 1190 and is surrounded on three sides by a tidal moat. It proved impregnable.

A lane-side bank in full flower near Lower Eweston, mid-May.

Wildflowers in profusion decorate a roadside bank near Solva in mid-May.

A tranquil moment in early summer at Bosherton Lily Ponds, now a National Nature Reserve.

Ffyst Samson, the remains of a Mesolithic burial chamber near St Nicholas Tremarchog.

Beside a green lane near St Nicholas Tremarchog, mid-May.

A standing stone at Ffynnon Druidion – the 'Druid's Spring' – near St Nicholas Tremarchog.

A Neolithic passage-grave of around 2500 BC, the cromlech of Carreg Samson stands overlooking the sea above Abercastle.

The church of St Brynach beside the Afon Nyfer at Nevern dates to the fifteenth century.

The Carew Cross dates to 1035 and commemorates Maredudd ap Edwin, a prince of Deheubarth – the far south western corner of Wales.

The imposing High Cross in St Brynach's churchyard at Nevern dates to the eleventh century.

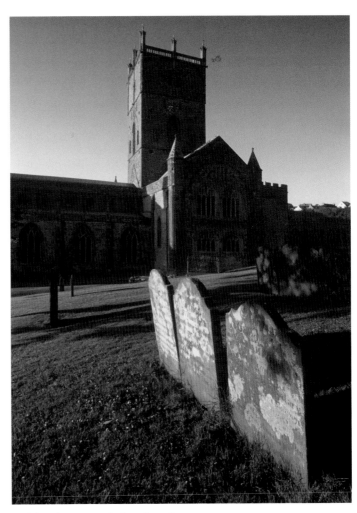

St David's Cathedral on a summer evening: left, the western aspect; right, the tranquil churchyard.

The stern-visaged Ebenezer Congregational Chapel at St David's dates to 1871 and stands on the hill overlooking the Cathedral.

This modern equivalent of an ancient standing stone stands beside the Pembrokeshire Coast National Trail.

This fragment of drystone wall above the Sound of Ramsay may well date to the Iron Age.

St Non's Holy Well, an ancient pilgrim halt, stands on the cliffs near St David's.

In this graphic composition the Cleddau Bridge frames the Texaco Rhoscrowther refinery on the far shore of Milford Haven.

MILFORD HAVEN AND THE CLEDDAU

Verdant green fields surround the great sail-scattered anchorage of Milford Haven – the flooded estuary of the River Cleddau. Little shoreside villages stand beside its inlets and bays where recreational sailors moor their craft. Keeping to the fairway, the leviathan tankers from distant waters ply to and from the oil and gas terminals. Beyond the high-striding bridge however, the Cleddau becomes a sinuous channel, twisting and turning between wooded shores until the tide reaches far into the hinterland. Secret creeks lead to abandoned quays and lonely cottages; a part of Pembrokeshire little known to outsiders.

High tide in Angle harbour, once a busy little port on Milford Haven but today a haven for yachtsmen.

The Pickleridge tidal lagoon at the head of Dale Roads.

On the Carew shore near Lawrenny Quay: sailing barges once plied the Daugleddau carrying anthracite coal from the long-abandoned mines which date to Tudor times.

Evening view from the beach at Dale across Dale Roads towards Musselwick Point.

Milford Haven: Texaco's Rhoscrowther refinery is seen against the sunset from the shore at Neyland.

Dusk view from Wallaston Cross of the Texaco oil refinery at Rhoscrowther on the southern shore of Milford Haven.

An outward-bound liquid-gas tanker proceeds down Milford Haven in this view across Dale Roads.

Evening light catches the imposing Cleddau Bridge which spans the entrance to the Daugleddau at the eastern end of Milford Haven in this view from Neyland waterfront.

The gentle eminence of Lawrenny Hill overlooks the confluence of the Creswell (left) and Carew (right) Rivers, divided at low tide by the reef of Black Mixen.

A boat lies moored in Black Mixen Pool where the Creswell meets the Carew River.

Autumn dawn over Dale Roads: a supertanker and the chimney of the Rhoscrowther oil refinery can be discerned in the distance left of the rising sun.

Still tidal, the Creswell River at the tiny hamlet of Creswell Quay.

Sailing down Castle Reach on the beautiful Daugleddau. The tower of Benton Castle rises from the autumnal woods.

Sailing dinghys on Dale Beach, a yachting centre near the mouth of Milford Haven. Great Castle Head is seen beyond.

Low tide at long-abandoned Landshipping Quay near the confluence of the Eastern and Western Cleddau.

The Eastern Cleddau extends deep inland: it is seen here, still tidal, near Landshipping Slip looking across to the charmingly-named Curlysky.

A small yacht runs down the Daugleddau on the tide. View northwards from Lawrenny Quay towards Beggar's Reach.

King's Quoit cromlech stands on the steep slopes of Priest's Nose above the shore in Manorbier Bay.

THE SOUTH COAST

Pembrokeshire's southern coast owes its character to the limestone from which it is largely composed. Bright and open, the cliff-tops smell in summer of wild thyme. Families enjoy seaside holidays at jolly Tenby, yet the town proudly retains a tasteful, slightly quaint Georgian atmosphere. Further west the highly stratified rock, light grey in colour and frequently twisted and distorted, forms miles of cliffs, never particularly high, broken by little sandy bays. It is a smiling shore that surely epitomises Little England beyond Wales.

The wide bay of Freshwater West: view northwards from Little Furzenip over the bay towards the dunes of Broomhill Burrows.

View southwards from Little Furzenip towards distant Linney Head, alas, part of the military reservation.

In this view from the clifftop above Skrinkle Haven the convoluted limestone cliffs of the southern coast stretch away towards Lydstep Point and distant Caldey Island.

An artist at work on the windswept crest of Lydstep Point.

Spectacular up-ended limestone strata on Whitesheet Rock, Lydstep Point.

78

Evening light on Manorbier Beach.

St Govan's Head is seen along a wall of sheer lime-stone cliffs.

Colourful cliffs near Sheep Island on the southern coast of the Angle Peninsula.

A natural arch and upended limestone strata at Skrinkle Haven, Lydstep.

The limestone cliffs of Proud Giltar rise some 150 feet above the north shore of Lydstep Haven.

In-coming tide at Broad Haven beach at the mouth of the little Bosherton river. Church Rock stands off-shore.

February sou'wester at Westdale Bay near St Ann's Head.

Mid-winter at the Green Bridge of Wales near Flimston Bay on the Castlemartin coast.

Gulls nest on the narrow summit of a sea-stack near Flimston Bay, Castlemartin coast.

Clumps of golden samphire on steep limestone cliffs near Flimston Bay, Castlemartin coast.

Caldy Island lies some two and a half miles east from Lydstep Point.

The Elugug Stacks: the higher stack was dubbed Elugug Tower.

The Elugug Stacks

The twin Elugug Stacks together with the nearby Green Bridge of Wales are probably the best-known features of the Castlemartin coast, whose cliffs have become one of the prime rock-climbing venues in Britain. We first discovered the stacks on a postcard in the late Sixties, when they were still very forbidden deep within the Army tank ranges. Busy exploring the rock-climbing potential of the Devon sea-cliffs at the time, we plotted an 'away' expedition to the far side of the Bristol Channel.

Permission was readily granted by the colonel commanding and, escorted by Red Caps, we finally reached the stacks on a November weekend in 1970. Their distinctive shapes immediately suggested the names Elugug Tower and Elugug Spire (above).

We abseiled into the little cove and in a fairly heavy sea swam out to the stacks and attached ropes for a 'Tyrolean traverse' – quite enough for a first reconnaissance.

Returning next day in better weather, we were able to reach the stacks via our traverse ropes dry-shod. Two members of the team climbed the imposing and plumb-vertical Spire, (pictures 1, 2 and 3 opposite) from whose loose and narrow summit they had to descend by a see-saw abseil – descending simultaneously, each on opposite faces to counter-balance the other. The rest of us climbed the Tower, a rather more mountaineering route of two pitches. But by late afternoon the weather had broken, the sea had risen and the tide was in. The abseil descent from a large clump of the sea-cabbages which crowned the Tower (picture 4) was followed by a good soaking as we were hauled back on our ropes through the surf to the mainland (picture 5).

1.   November 2, 1970. Ian Howell on the steep west face of the Elugug Spire.

2. The summit – first ascent of the Spire.

3.   Frank Cannings and Ian Howell on the narrow summit of the Spire. They descended together by counter-balanced abseil.

4. The tide rises and the weather worsens as climbers descend from the Tower. Pete Biven is last down.

5. The final return to the cliff bottom by Tyrolean traverse.

Tenby : the Lifeboat Station, Castle Hill and the colourful buildings on St Julian's Terrace rise over the harbour in this view from North Beach.

The elegant properties on St Julian's Terrace look down on Tenby Harbour in this view from the Mayor's Slip.

Victoria Street, Tenby off the Esplanade.

Handsome Georgian properties, Rock Terrace numbers 4 and 3, St Julian's Street, Tenby.

'Tides Reach' and 'Grey Rock', terraced houses in St Julian's Street, are characteristic of Georgian Tenby.

A typical neat B&B establishment.

Low tide at Tenby Harbour.

A colourful pub on Upper Frog Street in Tenby town centre.

Cheerful décor is a characteristic of Tenby's seaside boarding houses such as this one in Southcliffe Street

The fragmentry fortress on Castle Hill, Tenby, dates to the thirteenth century.

The narrow rocky headland of Dinas Fach juts into St Bride's Bay near Solva.

THE WEST COAST

Known as St Bride's Bay, the west coast, while open to the Irish Sea, is sheltered between the arms of the Marloes and Dewisland peninsulas. Wide sands and low cliffs broken by sheltered inlets line the bay with a scattering of little villages, while the twin headlands, reaching out towards the off-shore islands of Skomer and Ramsey, become craggy and the shores more rocky and wild. Access to the cliff-girt islands themselves, protected as wildlife havens, is across treacherous, tide-ripped sounds.

Secluded Porthmynawyd Cove is sheltered by the craggy promontory of Dinas Fach.

Summer sunset over North Bishop islet from St Justinian's. Ramsey Island and the rocky islets of Bishops and Clerks on the left.

Young hikers on the Coast Path descend the Gribin ridge towards the little harbour village of Solva.

Surf kayaking in Whitesands Bay below St David's Head.

Evening view over Porthstinian anchorage on Ramsey Sound, Ramsey island lies on the far right.

A hiker on the Coast Path climbs out of Gwaden Cove onto the Gribin Ridge above Solva.

View up the rocky coast of St Bride's Bay towards Newgale Sands.

The colourful main street of Solva village by the harbour.

Summer evening on St Bride's Bay – view from Maidenhall Point towards the islets of Black and Green Scar and Carn Llidi beyond.

Evening view near Porthlysgi Bay over the Carreg yr Esgob skerries to distant Ynys Bery and the southern tip of Ramsey.

This jolly gazebo under the Welsh Dragon overlooks Ramsey Sound at St Justinian's.

Falling tide on the long beach at Newgale Sands on St Bride's Bay. Rickets Head stands in the far distance.

The island of Skokholm, two and a half miles distant, is seen from Skomer Head on Skomer.

Skomer: vistors hike from the jetty to the island HQ in the old farm building at the centre of the island. Some of the field walls may date to the Iron-Age.

Rugged cliffs rise over 200 feet near the northernmost point of Skomer.

Off the north coast of Skomer.

Skomer: view across South Haven towards The Neck promontory and the mainland beyond.

A Skomer view northwards over St Bride's Bay.

Running Ramsey Sound, notorious for its tide race –The Bitches. Foel Fawr, the southern tip of Ramsey, and Ynys Cantwr island lie beyond.

Evening view from Ynys Dinas near St Justinian's towards the islets of North Bishop, some four miles distant.

115

Puffin on Skomer.

Visitors embark on the Skomer tender for the short return voyage to Martin's Haven.

In early summer much of Skomer is covered in red campion.

The wide sands of Traeth Llyfn near Porthgain

THE NORTH COAST

Pembrokeshire's northern shore is a essentially a Welsh coast, its bold personality very different from that of the smiling south. This is a rugged coast, fierce, craggy, broken and open to the weather. Here there are tall cliffs and tiny inlets, small beaches and offshore skerries, natural arches and twisted strata of dark rock. Bracken and heather carpet many a cliff top while small, strange hills, miniature mountains in style, rise in places above the shore and lend shape to the land. While a few small fishing craft work out of deep sheltered inlets such as Porthgain and Abercastle, such places are few on this long coast. In some thirty miles there are only two good harbours, Fishguard and Newport, both in river mouths protected behind major headlands. This north coast is Pembrokeshire in the raw.

The original Fishguard harbour lies in the tidal mouth of the Afon Gwaun at Lower Town. Not surprisingly it has been the location for several films, among them Dylan Thomas's *Under Milk Wood* in 1971.

The tiny haven of Porth Clais was the medieval harbour for St David's. View up the inlet from the breakwater.

For centuries the church of St Brynach stood on the foreshore at secretive Cwm-yr-Eglwys — the valley of the church — on Newport Bay. It was destroyed in the great storm of 1859, leaving only the remains of the tower, crowned now with a salmon weathervane and a peaceful, flower-filled churchyard at the water's edge.

The tranquil estuary of the Afon Nyfer near Newport. May.

The secluded harbour of Porth Clais in its deep inlet, the mouth of the Afon Alun, was much frequented in ancient times by pilgrims making their way by sea to nearby St David's.

Porpoise and Welsh Dragon at low tide in Porth Clais.

Sea-kayakers emerge from a deep cave in the cliffs at Porth Dwgan near Aberbach.

126

Navigating the Carreg Golchfa skerries off Porth Dwgan.

Powerful tides swirl round this skerry below Penbwchdy on the Strumble peninsula.

Wild flowers in mid-May on the rocky Penbwchdy Headland.

Interesting geology – a fine example of an anticline – is seen at low tide in Pwllcrochan cove near St Nicholas.

Craggy Garn Fawr rises over the dark, inaccessible cove of Pwll Deri. The white cottage is the remote Tal-y-Gaer youth hostel on the Coast Path.

An angry winter sea at the Carreg Wylan stacks off Caibwr Bay near Moylgrove.

Winter seas pound Ynys Fach and the 200 foot cliffs at Caibwr Bay near Moylgrove.

Low tide at Abercastle: fishermen still operate from this tiny haven.

One-time fishermen's cottages on the foreshore at Aber Eiddy north of St David's.

The village of Newport and its castle lie below the slopes of Carn Ingli in this view across the Nyfer estuary.

The old folly of Abereiddi Tower with Penberry Hill and Carn Llidi in the distance are seen over the bay of Traeth Llyfn.

The peaceful little anchorage at Cwm-yr-Eglwys, hidden at the base of Dinas Island.

The rugged west coast of the Strumble Peninsula: view from Dinas Mawr headland towards Pen Brush.

This page and opposite: In these views looking north from Carn Ingli Common, the green headland of Pen-y-Bal is seen across Newport Bay. Beyond the headland, eight miles of rugged cliffs, broken only by the inlet at Ceibwr, extend to Cemaes Head and the mouth of the Teifi at Cardigan.

This is the Pembrokeshire Coast Path above precipitous Pwll Deri cove on the west coast of the Strumble Peninsula. Penbwchdy Head on the far left.

The conspicuous lighthouse on Strumble Head is seen from the summit of Garn Fawr at 699 ft (213m) above Pwll Deri.

Granite and slate were once exported as far as London from the little harbour of Porthgain.

Summer season at Porthgain's tiny harbour.

Low tide in the old Lower Town harbour at Fishguard , the mouth of the Afon Gwaun.

Evening on Newport Sands with Dinas Head beyond.